THE BULLY-PROOF CLASSROOM

THE BULLY-PROOF CLASSROOM

AVERY NIGHTINGALE

CONTENTS

1	Introduction	1
2	Understanding Bullying	3
3	Recognizing the Signs	5
4	Creating a Safe Environment	7
5	Establishing Clear Expectations	9
6	Teaching Empathy and Compassion	11
7	Promoting Positive Relationships	13
8	Teaching Conflict Resolution Skills	15
9	Encouraging Open Communication	17
10	Fostering Inclusivity and Diversity	19
11	Addressing Cyberbullying	21
12	Building Resilience	23
13	Empowering Bystanders	25
14	Implementing Anti-Bullying Policies	27
15	Collaborating with Parents and Guardians	29
16	Providing Support for Victims	31
17	Training Staff and Faculty	33

18	Utilizing Restorative Practices	35
19	Promoting Social Emotional Learning	37
20	Creating a Positive School Climate	39
21	Implementing Peer Mediation Programs	41
22	Promoting Positive Behavior	43
23	Teaching Emotional Regulation	45
24	Supporting Mental Health	47
25	Addressing Bullying in Physical Education	49
26	Incorporating Bullying Prevention in the Curriculu	51
27	Using Technology to Address Bullying	53
28	Empowering Student Leaders	55
29	Evaluating and Monitoring Bullying Prevention Effo	57
30	Celebrating Diversity and Inclusion	59
31	Promoting a Culture of Respect	61
32	Conclusion	63

Copyright © 2024 by Avery Nightingale
All rights reserved. No part of this book may be reproduced in any manner whatsoever without written permission except in the case of brief quotations embodied in critical articles and reviews.
First Printing, 2024

CHAPTER 1

Introduction

In The Bully-Proof Classroom, author Caltha Crowe declares that today's children have repeatedly placed her in the embarrassing and intolerable position of enduring unstructured, unfettered, unlimited, and unrepentant bullying and harassment. To the point where school becomes a sick, vicious closed system that stinks and infects all of its inhabitants, and the support for the bully shuts down and crushes the bullied child or teacher. Crowe advances the theory that as our U.S. culture has moved from one that was inherently respectful of all to one in which some are honored and others expendable in the pursuit of enrichment, protection, and superiority, the discourse among all of us reflects and perpetuates these attitudes.

While Crowe's endnotes support her contention that less and less discourse in our community at large is civil and engenders mutual respect, she borrows the examples from her own emotionally abusive career as an elementary, middle, and high school music educator, an ethnomusicologist, and as a psychotherapist daughter of parents born in the 1920s, both of whom were also educators. Crowe develops an essential question and four subsidiary questions that she addressed in the various studies. All of the studies drew attention to the excruciating anguish that children endured as they became isolated from both classmates and teachers by bullying and harassment in our schools. The book constitutes her response to them. It also illustrates her method of teaching kindness, self-control, and compassionate recognition of others in balance so that all students develop a sense of themselves as honest, responsible, sympathetic, humorous, patient, openly joyful, free-spirited, resourceful, focused, radiantly beautiful individuals – rather than as victims or mediocrities.

CHAPTER 2

Understanding Bullying

But increasingly, more and more school personnel have begun to understand that having an anti-bullying program in their schools is very different from having a school that has a culture of respect, where bullying is not tolerated and where adults have very different ways of receiving and reacting to reports of bullying than they do in schools that "only" have an anti-bullying program in place. Just as important, we are learning that the reluctance to fully implement strategies aimed at preventing bullying are present not only in schools, but also among many adults who view their approach to work through colloquial lenses - "He'll learn to toughen up." These prolonged misconceptions increase the difficulties many children who are bullied continue to encounter, long after their encounters in school where they initially received no protection from their classmates or their adult supervisors.

From the outside, the strategies we teach, such as encouraging students and teachers to report bullying incidents and ensuring that bullies understand that their actions are unacceptable, appear to be working. After all, how often these days do we hear about adults who were bullied at the hands of their classmates in school?

Many schools are grappling with ways of dealing successfully with bullying. Most states now have laws aimed at preventing bullying, harassment, and cyber-bullying in public schools. And in the past 12 years, the Massachusetts Aggression Reduction Center (MARC) at Bridgewater State University has trained thousands of teachers, school administrators, and school resource officers in successfully implementing anti-bullying programs and strategies to help prevent bullying and cyber-bullying.

Brown Bear thought he would teach Shark a lesson about teasing. He crowed, "Hiya! I'm the biggest, baddest bully of the sea!" But Giant Squid told him that he was wrong. "You can't be a bully, Brown Bear! You are only kidding. You know better than to scare such an itsy-bitsy fish like Shark."

CHAPTER 3

Recognizing the Signs

Other signs of potential bullying include depression, loneliness, anxiety, and difficulty in school. In general, victims of bullying feel that nobody sees them, especially in situations outside of the classroom. They often refuse to go to restrooms, and if they do go, they lock the door. It is essential for teachers to intervene and defend these students to deny the bully of the negative attention the student craves.

Victims of bullying are emotionally very sensitive. Students who often have rashes on their arms may be victims of bullying. Often, while I am lecturing, I have noticed students who cannot stop drawing on their arms. When you look at what they are drawing, you realize that it is a series of names or words. The pain they feel as a result of the repetitive abusive behavior makes them want to feel physical pain instead of emotional pain.

Signs of potential bullying include children who act very disrespectfully. They refuse to listen to others' point of view and constantly correct their peers when answering a question or providing an explanation. In addition, they mimic teachers' words or those of other students in a disrespectful way. Bullies are very good at transforming their victims into the worst person in the classroom. For example, if a student does not follow the line formed outside the classroom door, bullies use that as an excuse to force the student to go last in line.

Unquestionably, some students become bullies because they have been bullied themselves. Bullying at school is often a group activity, with bystanders feeding the bully when they vicariously endorse the bullying behavior. Yet this does not happen only among children; research shows that teachers who believe they are being victimized by their supervisors often turn around and display anger and frustration with their students.

CHAPTER 4

Creating a Safe Environment

This enforcement, however, is more effective within a zero-tolerance policy. Reminiscent of the secular principle of deterrence, zero tolerance portrays an atmosphere less receptive to aggression, with trickles of applause aimed at those who dare to defend the weak. However, just the legality of such policies has been criticized if it doesn't accommodate particular circumstances. Stipulated frameworks aren't always supportive. But the same net, cast upon therapeutic and punitive strategies, also limits unhealthy classroom interactions, stimulating cohesion and empathy among students, whether among teachers. Consistent and communal in application, educators upon transforming the promise of such policies into reality commit a leap across the space-time continuum, much like astronauts, successfully merging the construction of decrees and administrative structures with the day-to-day activity and essence of good relationships. Eye contact and conscious listening shape communication, with faculty within the bully-proof classroom considering their own actions compassionate and empathic. Assistant faculty promptly inform denies her own oppressive behavior towards a student her authority, preventing unchecked abuse of second-class citizens. Such norms regulate interaction and daily engagements while maintaining the student's respect for every other community member, eradicating any tension or confusion over what is or is not acceptable behavior.

Safe schools convey a message of caring, warmth, and tolerance through both physical and emotional comfort. Physical comfort is experienced through a multilevel approach to ease minor problems, such as dimming a flickering light that may provoke irritability. In contrast, emotional comfort is supported by clear rules and regulations, a moral tone, and a commonly enforced system of rewards. Moreover, creating a climate of support through relationships shared among staff, parents, and students can relieve some of the stress, making tight-knit communities more resilient and capable of adapting to challenging situations. Consequently, it's within schools' capacity to minimize emotional concerns and construe adopting the premises of a bully-proof classroom less of a task and more characteristic of preventive measures worthy of universal application.

CHAPTER 5

Establishing Clear Expectations

Teachers who are consistent in their enforcement of rules are their students' most effective weapon against bullies. Some key aspects of our no-tolerance policy on acts of disrespect are: using a formal discipline method that includes conferencing and contacting parents to ensure that students understand the seriousness of their actions; giving students the chance to apologize to the wronged party, not merely make excuses for their behavior; and informing administrators when the degree of harassment reaches the level at which bullying is considered a category 3 violation. We note incidents for future reference and act as soon as we see a pattern developing. Our goal is to establish the norms of polite society in our class while teaching students the importance of being compassionate citizens who accept responsibility for their actions. During the past two years, only two of my high school students, neither of whom is currently in this class, have been involved in serious cases of hazing. It worked!

In a bully-proof classroom, there is no doubt about what is expected in terms of proper manners, behavior, or treatment of others. The establishment of classroom rules is integral to this environment.

Students will respect teachers who enforce rules fairly and hold those who disregard them responsible for their actions. These basic expectations establish the norms of respect and courtesy that should be indicative of all interactions in the class, both among students and between student and teacher. Teachers and students working in bully-proof classrooms hold their peers to high standards of behavior. They do not let hurtful or abusive comments pass unnoticed. Rather, they make it a point to confront the person who has crossed the line and let him or her know such statements are unacceptable.

CHAPTER 6

Teaching Empathy and Compassion

As read-alouds are conducted, read the reactions of the different characters in the story and begin by identifying the character in the book that is not contributing as they should. Be direct with reminding the class that whether the characters in the book can properly engage does not shift the expectation of your students to respect the class. Bring meaning into the hearts of students with classroom activities that have them thinking about their place, perceived and original, within their community. It is necessary to facilitate conversations about altruistic service and positive peer interaction, sometimes shuffling, in order to modify incorrect negative judgments thus providing a progressive learning environment filled with kindness and compassion. Regularly validating the responses of students sharing experiences or thoughts that show kindness is essential. Limiting or minimizing undesirable responses in these circumstances are better left corrected through opportunities surrounding classroom respect between students versus being communicated in the act of compassion from one student to another.

Not all students know how to recognize and identify the needs, feelings, and concerns of others. These structures act as guides during discussions from book characters who deal with concerns affecting your students ranging from embarrassing moments to general acts of kindness. Books with great rapport between the characters provide good examples for your students of how acts of kindness can impact others. When discussing the stories, focus on the words or acts of kindness that helped another individual as well as how the situation made the characters feel. Identify the roles of different characters and connect those roles with types of behavior in real life. Act out different scenarios with hypothetical characters who represent your class. Time should be allocated for the re-enactments. It is important also to provide models of interacting with others in order to demonstrate what to do and assist children with inferring what they can do themselves. Begin with the teacher first modeling empathy with students and with others ever present. Not only in this role modeling but also in general, adults must send consistent messages to children that empathy is valued.

CHAPTER 7

Promoting Positive Relationships

A warm, involved teacher is a bulwark against this sort of thing happening. This is so because an experienced teacher effectively pulls students away from the hostile culture that is so much a part of young people's lives to a different kind of culture, one that yearns for healing for those who are wounded by society and begins to dispel the feeling that hope itself is dead. When a positive environment has been established within the classroom, teachers need to make their expectations known that students will adhere to created class standards and guidelines. If this is not implemented, the rules and guidelines that teachers expect students to uphold will bear little or no weight or authority. And if the rules have little weight, the developmental progress of the students will be forfeited as well, just as a sound education would be forfeited if rules of teaching were nonexistent, unclear, or inconsistently enforced.

Students are less likely to bully and demean each other if they are part of a community of classmates who are united in spirit and purpose, and who have formed healthy, mutually respectful, and emotionally supportive relationships with their teacher and with each other. Teachers need to be proactive to ensure that such a family-centered ambiance is firmly established from the first day of school. If teachers are delinquent and fail to foster a spirit of community, they have made no one responsible for the character development of the students in their charge. The danger is that a totally negative environment will be created, one that is full of strife, backbiting, and unfairness and that is certainly not focused on the welfare and support of the members themselves.

CHAPTER 8

Teaching Conflict Resolution Skills

1) A growth in the number of reported instances of bullying is emerging in all levels of schools. Bullying always results in harm, distress, and even death and may have long-term disruptive consequences on each person concerned. Victims of bullying may suffer from low self-esteem, parent-child communication, and physical health problems. On the other hand, the bullies may grow to be grown-up abusers or offenders or assume a bad mental state themselves. Others, like onlookers, can often experience cognitive distress as a consequence of associating themselves with the bullying at any stage. It is apparent that the culture of bullying triggers both direct and long-range distress to each person concerned. Educators are literally in the act of engaging with students, and through enjoyable, friendly learning environments, they can certainly teach them to demonstrate respect for the individuality and variations among people.

2) Because not all schools have regular classes in social and (peer) conflict-solving instruction, it is convenient to assume that some pupils may not have the sufficient social and communicative abilities to intervene themselves in tough problems. This is known as the ex-

tremely important ability of intervention. In order to communicate with people, pupils with severe behavioral problems should undergo thorough and intensive training. To discuss their thoughts sympathetically, thoroughly, and without reproach, they also require monitoring of the warning signs behind the behavior. We work with a fundamental conflict-resolution structure and advise both parties to acknowledge their difficulty and then imagine how the encounter has contributed to negative thoughts, feelings, or behaviors. For instance, it is beneficial to indicate event maps or lists the important activities experienced by each group as well as planning what events may happen in any specific order and the seriousness of their effect on both parties' wellness in order to make pupils visualize the situation.

CHAPTER 9

Encouraging Open Communication

Student hesitancy urging direct communication with the teacher reveals itself in multiple forms ranging from a single question posed through a shy smile to the paper-and-pen responses reluctantly handed to the teacher with brief "Can you answer my question?" Although the initial poem or sentence might not meet the expectations, analyzing it provides the information necessary for the path leading to clear classroom communication. The teacher must diffuse the tension between her answers paving the path the shy children will launch their brave, albeit shy, answers. Praise delivered through a sincerely-expressed smile and open body language persuades all students to synthesize information coined verifiable by whatever interpretation fits. Resounding applause celebrates every correct response, but also allows any naïve interpretations to play themselves out in communal questioning and answers. The process concludes when the students request an explanation, regard their interpretations as belonging to them, and reshape their responses to match more precisely precise explanations, externally and mutually determined as correct. Slickly, students transform themselves from hesitant communicators internalizing a shamed secrecy to confident students demanding attention through the sincerity revealing active behavior. All students eagerly record and share responses to every assignment placed before them. Their answers amass columns after columns as the examination requires the students to align them in organized lines, the meticulous records serving as the class objectives until the next test.

Small voices murmur "I'm scared" and "Nobody likes me," and "She calls me mean names." Unconsciously, children become hesitant participants in class discussions. These whispers deny the emotional turbulence swirling below the smooth surface of the classroom environment. The voices vary in timbre and volume from the smallest whisper to the loudest outburst, but silence indicates profound fear. Removing the obstacles inhibiting classroom communication strengthens the students' bonds, rendering the resulting group as invincible as Redwood trees. A teacher can amplify the number of individuals expressing honest, candid emotions with both the tone of her verbal and nonverbal messages and the way she organizes her class.

CHAPTER 10

Fostering Inclusivity and Diversity

Even the short biographies that highlight the lived experiences of leaders or groups throughout history in the resources that you share can serve as a critical entry point into a bigger conversation. You might invest brief minutes of time meant for this purpose into conversations in a daily or weekly "activist spotlight," or so to speak, especially among the materials that you choose to share. Encourage broad conversations about the big biographies (and important, though perhaps less well-known figures who have nonetheless made considerable impacts) that do not often surface when discussing topics like the civil rights movement in the unit. Highlight accomplishments not only from the many known white leaders of the era, but also accomplishments of the black community, or else portray a myriad of unsung individuals who have made great sacrifices for the greater good over the course of the United States' history. Published primary sources might also represent opportunities for meaningful exploration of diversity, particularly as led by a caption beneath noting the silenced voices highlighted within privileged, and overly white, perspectives during moments of upheaval.

Classroom interactions have the capacity to shape how children view themselves and others. That much is clear by any cursory observation taken of the remarks shared by students inside of the classroom. However, pushing our students towards greater capacities for empathy and understanding of those unlike themselves requires intentionality. Throughout our work this year, we'll push students of all ages to think carefully about the power of their words and actions and to find meaningful ways to make connections with unlikely allies. These exercises are meant to build a lasting culture of respect and question harmful biases and tropes early and often. Engage students in conversations about a diverse canon of scholars and humanitarians in the lessons that you design.

CHAPTER 11

Addressing Cyberbullying

Our school pledges to keep both our bodies and minds safe. We promise to also guard our thoughts and personal information to ensure that we stay within our own safety zones. The elementary school community has agreed to assist me in maintaining my online safety, and in return, I will support others by promoting safety awareness.

There are ample opportunities for students to collaborate on creating safety in the school community through class meetings, school assemblies, and individual conversations with teachers and peers. Kindergarteners are capable of creating detailed solutions when identifying what frightens them. Teach preschool and elementary students to protect personal information both online and offline by developing the policy with them. Additionally, let these students know who and when to tell if they are approached inappropriately either online or offline.

As an example, students in 4th grade contribute the following when creating the anti-web safety harassment poster: examples that they identify are to "not give your address or phone number on the internet; do not open emails from people you do not know; I don't give out my passwords; kill as-blocks; when I go to share, I do not give out my last name, only my first name and sometimes not my middle name; I don't tell anyone that I do not know and if even I do not want to; I can't and I won't talk to anyone online if it's my first meeting; always give a fake address or phone number if you have to; my password keeps me safe; keep the personal information safe, so nobody can come and get me."

In creating the bully-proof classroom, a top priority is developing a school culture of respect that encourages student web safety and respects all people. It is also necessary to empower students to stay safe, keep personal information safe, and to protect themselves when web safety is threatened. Personal information may include sensitive personal information such as private addresses, telephone numbers, family financial information, school information, and photographs.

CHAPTER 12

Building Resilience

Do not focus on how individual students can improve grades, but focus on how collective academic potential can be grown when one person helps another. Use the concept of the "zone of proximal development" often experimented with in a collaborative learning environment to help the students understand that helping others will enhance the helper's internal understanding of subjects and overall abilities.

Make sure that every student is aware that everyone in the room will be receiving both attention and accountability. Require that no one remain anonymous or alone, and make sure that every student is linked to at least one adult in the school. Normalize help-seeking behaviors.

Make sure that you are providing regular feedback that is instructional in all areas of life, not just academic work. Teach students that failure is only failure if you don't learn from the experience, and repeat the experiences in a new way. Celebrate taking risks and making new choices.

Make sure that students understand how the old brain, or brain stem, takes over during times of fight or flight and often overrides more sophisticated thinking centers of the brain. Analogies and honest discussions will go far in helping them to understand that although they are not always in complete control of those times, they can still shape their responses. This basic biological information will also help them understand why it may be important to help abusers as they perform abusive behaviors.

The goal of bully-proofing the classroom is to create a sense of physical and emotional safety for everyone, and this can ultimately be achieved only if we are assisting our students in enhancing their own resilience skills. (Resilience is the capacity to rise above difficult circumstances, sustenance in the face of adversity, and the ability to achieve well-being in the face of trauma, physical illness, or depression.) Their resilience skills will help students stop ruminating over negative events and focus on problem solving, recognize when they need to seek help in managing their strong emotions, and increase their overall frustration tolerance, while improving self-esteem and self-regulatory abilities. Positive, incremental, nurturing, and non-competitive feedback taps into the brain's reward center, and growth/performance data (and therefore letter grades) can serve as more of a negative reinforcer for behaviors such as cheating and competition with peers. Here are some ways in which we build resilience in the classroom:

CHAPTER 13

Empowering Bystanders

Reminder labels can also serve as cues to students to use the phone numbers when abusive situations or individuals are imminent. Role modeling other ways in which students can help can also be useful. Instead of being a passive fragment in a larger chain of injustice, a child can increase his ethereal value by supporting another person or helping. Children can also build a variety of personal attributes by helping others, ones that will stay with them moments more lasting than any bullying incidents.

Students should have a list of phone numbers both in people in school with whom they can talk and outside the school. This information can be found in telephone books, online, or from personal conversations with parents or relatives. Phone numbers can be kept compact by using symbols or writing, sparsely filling in what is known. Younger children may need to realize that people abuse their positions of authority, hence, often the best adults to approach are those who are not in the direct line of authority.

A successful model for bystander education consists of a number of principles. These include identifying one's responsibility, educating what to look for, and understanding how to help. Studies indicate that the act of a single person within a bully chain system is what will ultimately lead to positive resolution, unless unacceptable behavior is confronted.

Bystanders are people who witness inappropriate behavior in others. There are generally three types of bystanders. The first type is passive, and this individual either does not realize any harm is being done or does not believe it is any of his business to intervene. A second type is the false positive bystander, who believes there might be a problem but has decided to avoid ownership or responsibility so as not to incur wrath or to be labeled by others as a rat. The third kind of bystander is the active bystander who, although not asked, offers help.

CHAPTER 14

Implementing Anti-Bullying Policies

At a minimum, these plans should require school staff to intervene in behavior they observe and train teachers to effectively intervene. Implementation can go beyond school staff with school psychologists, parents, community leaders, and local law enforcement to address bullying at school. Included in school behavior plans should be rules for students to understand survey behavior bullying and consequences. Unlike the order of a school-wide behavior plan, data, and communication, each requires little to no school funds. Redistributions, however, involve organizing community resources to enforce the plan. Bowllan cues, a public school administrator in Brooklyn, suggests parents invite experts in the field regarding bullying and other safety topics that are important to families and school staff.

Over the past two decades, the United States has passed many resources aimed at lessening the prevalence of bullying in schools. The National Center for Educational Statistics reported in 2015 that 21 percent of students reported being bullied, and 15 percent said they were cyberbullied, during the school year. Prior to embracing a comprehensive program like the 3 Rs mentioned in the previous page, schools must pass school-wide behavior plans to combat bullying. EducationWorld offers a guide to writing these plans that covers safety assessment, data keeping, setting clear and administrative expectations, clear rules for students, and implementation. A study by Lynette Feder, at the University of Illinois, found these plans to be the most reliable in preventing bullying.

CHAPTER 15

Collaborating with Parents and Guardians

The following activities are "designed to facilitate a partnership with parents and guardians grounded in respect," says Dr. Kimberly D. Brown, winner of the 2009 Ken Fantroy Humanitarian Award for National Advocacy in Education. Empowerment activities for parents and guardians such as "Empowered Parents Behind School Reform," which helped parents in an urban district receive the assistance, documents, and strategies they needed to make informed decisions about choosing a magnet program for their child, are also proposed. "We, as educators, do not prepare children to compete with one another in the job market. We prepare them to be able to collaborate, discuss problems during peer work, and ask questions," says Brown. Therefore, collaboration between all stakeholders is beneficial. "The academic outcomes for children whose parents are involved are better when parents are involved in the process. We have an ethical obligation to provide empowerment activities open to all parents, even the parents of children who our policies might not be designed to accommodate."

In today's diverse classrooms, collaboration between parents/guardians and the schools that educate their children is especially important during the K-12 years. To counter the fragmented communication that often occurs between culturally diverse schools and families, educators and school administrators need a variety of resources to foster strong partnerships. These resources should be respectful, encourage communication, and highlight the valuable contributions all play in the successful education of our nation's children. The purpose of this chapter is to identify and explore eight initiatives and activities that educators and school administrators can use to collaboratively engage a variety of schools, and the families they serve, in the process of increasing respect, bullying prevention/stopping, and other social justice issues that critically impact schools and society.

CHAPTER 16

Providing Support for Victims

In the end, supervision is crucial and should not be ignored. Addressing rational desires and disappointments is important. Understand that victims who feel unsafe may be hesitant to come forward. If possible, assure your classmates that individuals who display anger and subjective behavior will be guided away from causing harm. Increase monitoring during break times, ensure kitchen equipment is handled safely during meal preparation, maintain security within the school building, and monitor automatic doors to ensure the safety of everyone. Coordinate laundry and cleaning activities before and during the school day. Encourage the reporting of both direct and indirect incidents.

Schools, parents, and communities must work together to help victims of bullying who have both immediate and long-term needs. General suggestions to assist victims are based on a collective understanding of feelings of upset and betrayal, fear and paranoia, negative attitudes towards their peers, and the loss of trust and friendships. Offer victims comfort, consolation, and support. Do not share secrets with victims, but instead be forgiving and sensitive to their needs. Approach victims with empathy to let them know that their experiences are valid and offer ways to support each other. Also, be vigilant for individuals who protect and comfort the victims.

CHAPTER 17

Training Staff and Faculty

Being so closely connected as colleagues and so thoroughly understanding the roles each of us plays (including how we influence the damage - or benefit - of being either an upstander or bystander as well as how we can reaffirm that a student's silence is a potentially dangerous strategy) was so invaluable that we even restructured our "team teaching" instruction to group by grade level rather than by discipline in order to be more available for each other on a regular basis. This kind of connectedness is an essential support for a program of a school of any kind but is also one of the most important things to maintain within a building when the original primary focus of the program (whether simply an excellent educational curriculum or a school feeling increasingly committed to responding to an immediate national educational concern such as behavior and conduct) is more commonly recognized in other communities outside one's own. While a lesson plan can be loaned or borrowed, models for a preventive classroom environment are only effective when it is very clear the team speaks with one voice.

What a powerful gift we give our students when we give them the gift of dignity - not only by giving it to them, but also by showing them how to give it to each other. What a rich environment we give them when we honor not only their voice, but also their silence.

What confident communicators we foster when we teach them both the power of language and the power of silence and how to use each effectively. We don't have to teach children how to speak; they come hardwired for that experience. We do, however, need to teach them how to communicate, and we can be better teachers to them in this way when we, ourselves, are better communicators. This is part of the cornerstone of our bullying prevention program at Barth Elementary School - an ongoing effort to communicate effectively with each other.

CHAPTER 18

Utilizing Restorative Practices

Forming partnerships with organizations within the community helps school communities collaborate to tackle bullying in more effective ways. It is recommended that schools foster relationships with organizations such as the Girl Scouts, Boy Scouts, communities of faith, and other schools. Reaching outside the school walls to outside partners can promote powerful impacts and outcomes. Such strategies help education and intervention efforts in a more impartial manner. IASP's (2012) "Benchmarks for School-wide Bullying Prevention (2nd ed.) Guide" encourages schools to work together, form partnerships with families, and include agencies such as mental health organizations. Such development and growth can greatly change the school environment. Students from the same neighborhood may have heard a story or two of local bullying prevention programs. Some mix physical and online (digital) communities to educate others. Such a diverse approach to improve physical bullying prevention efforts includes community members, teachers, and high school students.

Utilizing restorative practices as part of a bullying prevention program is important. When one abuses a person, one also abuses the community in which that person belongs. By responding to harm in ways that restore and forgive and by focusing on three simple, yet powerful questions—What happened? Who has been harmed? What needs to happen to make it right?—a community can heal, learn, and grow. Restorative justice in schools can involve a range of practices including restorative conferences, restorative circles, restorative mediation, and peer juries. Restorative approaches also help schools encourage adult authority, ensure the safety of every school community member, and empower school and community leaders to recognize and repair harm. These practices are easily implemented and are cost-effective. They are also valuable because they encourage empathy for the victim, justice, and for the parties involved to learn from the incident and to be accountable. While restorative practices are currently evidence-based interventions, according to the U.S. Department of Justice, Office of Justice Programs, the use of restorative practices is still in the early stages and requires further examination and assessment. However, there are no limits to their use, and schools can form strong community partnerships with other organizations that share a similar vision.

CHAPTER 19

Promoting Social Emotional Learning

Social emotional learning (SEL) has been identified as one of the major factors that reduces bullying and reduces the severity of the bullying that does occur. The Collaborative for Academic, Social, and Emotional Learning (CASEL), the organization that champions SEL principles, has identified five core competencies that exemplify a supportive and respectful classroom environment: self-awareness, self-management, responsible decision-making, relationship skills, and social awareness. Research confirms that when our students are competent in these areas they are less likely to bully others, and they are less likely to be victimized by bullies. Moreover, children who receive classroom instruction in SEL are statistically less likely to experience emotional distress, engage in physical fighting, and attribute hostility to others. Finally, a meta-analysis of studies conducted by the Collaborative for Academic, Social, and Emotional Learning shows that SEL programs conducted in schools improve students' attitudes and behaviors.

It's time for some good news: bullying is preventable. With more than two decades of bullying research and experience under our belts, we now know how to sow the seeds of violence and why they grow. What's needed now are school administrators and teachers who are willing to dig them up before they get started. This work has created a brighter future for everyone, because what benefits those most in need, benefits everyone.

CHAPTER 20

Creating a Positive School Climate

Take the sometimes conflicting policies created in the last five years. Many state houses have crafted regulations that require their schools to develop anti-bullying curricula, and an increasing number of states have created laws requiring character education in their schools. At the same time, the No Child Left Behind law has created the impetus for states to design guidelines to promote effective school discipline. And within the last year, the federal government has created "safe schools" benchmarks to be included as a part of its criteria for monitoring the behavior of states. These benchmarks were not only in line with state-created benchmarks, which require schools to aspire to provide a caring community, but also with the federal referendum on effective school discipline. United States Secretary of Education Margaret Spellings not only looked to the benchmarks as important overall indicators about our country's educational environments, but also determined that compared to school performance, judging a school's success is possible on safety matters alone.

Educational researchers and policymakers have increasingly turned their focus to the connection between well-disciplined schools and student achievement. Classroom management, which includes the traditional and much-studied behaviors teachers use to control their students, is one important aspect of classroom discipline. But researchers are now looking beyond classroom management to explore how teachers can play a role in shaping a schoolwide climate that puts the behavior of all its inhabitants in a positive light. Moreover, educational policy is beginning to reflect the understanding that reducing bullying is essential for creating well-disciplined schools and for improving student achievement.

CHAPTER 21

Implementing Peer Mediation Programs

The primary responsibility of adults in early education is to guide problem-solving during activities and social interactions. In these situations, adults can act when witnessing dangerous, severely destructive, or teacher-intolerant behavior. In classrooms, on playgrounds, and during transit to and from school, good models of language used in polite requests are mostly effective in guiding the social behavior of children. Resolving conflicts by letting children explain themselves, synthesizing the stories given, and articulating problems in simple sentences lead to resolutions by the children rather than by adults. A classroom community where people respect and help each other contrasts with a most peculiar tribunal, which supports conflict resolution by typically treating only the complaints of those who cannot resolve conflicts themselves. In a safe environment that builds integrity concurrently with esteem, children begin to cultivate data gathering and problem-solving skills.

In a good many situations, elementary and middle school students can resolve conflicts between their peers easily. Training is necessary for effective peer mediators, however. Mediation is ineffective if mediators solve the participants' problem for them. Mediation does not require agreement between the disputants, just clarification and understanding of the problem. Although mediators should articulate rules for problem-solving situations, mediators often are effective by asking participants what they intend to do. The training involves emotional and social awareness, so that a child might understand his or her feelings and those of others, so that a child might reason and make decisions, and so that a child might begin constructive conversations. Even children who are trained only to be peacekeepers learn to deal with minor conflicts, though not more serious disagreements.

CHAPTER 22

Promoting Positive Behavior

Despite the abundance of anti-bullying programs and the best efforts of professionals, it is disheartening that things don't always get better. What are we missing? This book provides a straightforward model for creating an environment which consistently promotes respectful behavior. It includes the practical, step-by-step procedures to address inappropriate behaviors that do occur. Such a comprehensive, proactive approach successfully addresses and manages a broad range of problematic social behaviors, including both "common classroom" incidents and more serious bullying episodes. This book helps the teacher directly and immediately influence and shape their own professional learning community: their classroom. Once our teachers and students come to agreements on classroom expectations, we have a way for children to hold one another accountable for being positive community members rather than friends and learning partners. With this shared vision in place, learning can flourish.

When parents drop off their little skeleton at school, they expect their child to be safe. That doesn't only mean physically, it means their emotional well-being as well. We educators understand this and we do everything in our power to protect our kids and make sure they are okay. Though students' safety is one of our greatest concerns, it's difficult to completely shield them. One of the most surprising aspects of teaching is realizing the extent of peer hostilities I witness daily. The nature of the teacher-student relationship means that I may be the only adult a child tells about the taunting they experienced during lunch, so I have to be both counselor and confidant. I'm the one that reports bullies to the administration, but I feel like the worst part is knowing that nothing will be done; that teacher apathy will make the situation even worse when the bullies find out who told.

CHAPTER 23

Teaching Emotional Regulation

The Kids of Violence study in the last chapter further proves that when kids and safe adults come together to create a culture of respect, children will respond with amazing results. Emily, who moved to Chicago from a small town in upstate New York, said she was amazed at the positive behavior at Schurz. This school was brought to her by fate. Emily was absolutely the right person to be with us. She knows just how to protect Kristine, Katie, Jamie, and Jose. She protects them to help protect all the other students in the class. I watched Emily embrace diversity. Emily naturally builds a community that respects race, faith, and ability. Emily advises her students, "If the speaker talking about another race is part of another race, then you can listen. If the speaker talking about another faith is part of another faith, then you can listen. If the speaker saying children with another ability can't do something is part of another ability, then you can listen." Emily walked by Jose the other day. While surrounding Katie with six feet of paper, bags, boxes, Kleenex, and Jamie, Emily was quick to praise Jose. She gasped, "Jose, can I take you home?!" I hadn't seen Jose that day but I braced myself. I use humor to my advantage, "You can take Emily if you take me!" I guess when I walked into the room with Jose, his shoulders were straight and he showed off his healthy tan!

The process helps a child build and sustain positive relationships, handle a crisis, and work out problems with other people. Involving children by asking them about their preferences while teaching or identifying potential choices at school are simple ways to build community. Embracing differences by talking about students and roles gives school community strength. Identifying positive qualities and talents helps students connect with each other in meaningful ways. These practices encourage all students to connect to a larger vision. They strive for that vision because it motivates them. In high school, kids take more responsibility for their world and actions. If they understand that they are responsible for the safe environment and they feel a connection to something greater than themselves, they strive to care for it.

How can a teacher teach emotional regulation to students who hurt other students? The 40 Developmental Assets are how. These assets can be learned. They are primarily taught by how one is treated. How teachers treat students and how school treats its community teaches kids how to behave. "Enjoying and valuing diversity" is one of the 40 Developmental Assets. Children who treat all people with respect are children who learn how to focus empathetically. Listen for a child's needs, ideas, and how she feels. Address the needs and ideas and honor the feelings. This process encourages self-awareness, self-regulation, empathy, and respect for others. This process creates emotional regulation. Emotional regulation leads to confidence in communicating.

CHAPTER 24

Supporting Mental Health

The impact on mental health also calls upon educators to understand how students who are victimized by aggressive behaviors may react to maintain a sense of control. There are plausible explanations for some of these responses. For example, gaslighting victimization was related to stonewalling as potential self-preservation strategies for youth who know they are being gaslit. Other research indicates that proactive aggressive individuals sometimes resort to cyberbullying when they think revenge and other reactance behaviors are acceptable. Knowing that reactive cowardly behaviors cause victimized students to be perceived as weak or socially isolated and cause other disruptive behaviors, and knowing that proactive aggression in individuals cannot prevent malicious humor unwisely used towards a minority in the school, teachers must not only try to prevent reactive coping strategies for their students but also know how to proactively earn the trust of victimized students.

Aggressive behaviors directly impact student mental health. Problems with bullying, behaviors causing disruption or threat, lower academic achievement, and feelings of isolation, alienation, or lack of support are all risk factors for depression in youth. In actuality, victimized students are more likely to experience either internalizing or externalizing mental health issues. Despite the fact that many teachers already manage supporting behavioral change with typical classroom interventions, victimized students report that teacher support was rare in classrooms, despite its frequency for uninvolved students. This difficult classroom agreement to both prevent the existence and impact of challenging behavior and manage it once it occurs leaves many teachers hoping for successful results while working with a victimized student, but not completely understanding how to achieve them.

CHAPTER 25

Addressing Bullying in Physical Education

Furthermore, those few minutes at the end of class satisfy or reinforce the criteria for leaders. So the physical education teacher is in a unique position to make exceptionally effective use of supervisory moments during class. As a teacher of the whole school's student body, the physical education teacher is a person of considerable influence. When this expertise is applied without fear or favor, students develop and exhibit respect, cooperation, and social skills. They also learn to develop responsible long-term relationships that improve the quality of their lives. Specifically aware of students who repeatedly skirt responsibilities, become absent without leave (truancy), or engage in misconduct, the physical education teacher affects the future of the school climate by making relevant reports. Although less likely perhaps to enact measures that can quickly reverse misconduct, the physical educator's lengthy knowledge base about learning and the variables associated with both acquisition and performance allows a rich understanding of the parameters or conditions that are maintaining developing maladaptive behavior in the usual school environment. This knowledge base, linked with a school environment that consistently embraces the principles of character education and practices them, will turn the tide and lead many score keepers and sellers into high achievers and leaders.

The physical education teacher plays a significant role in controlling bullying. While no teacher has the time to be everywhere, physical educators have a great opportunity to reduce the amount of teasing, taunting, and threats between students. Periodically, they are the teacher in charge of 50 to 100 students, all in one place, all at the same time. Usually, they are in a large space, and those with good instructional strategies can effectively reduce potential problems by manipulating the size and ability of groups, offering activities appropriate to the developmental level and skill of students, providing consistent instruction and rules, and practicing responsible behavior. They often have the undivided attention of students when reporting scores, discussing the rules of a game, and preparing to further explain rules. Most students understand that the few minutes between activities are valuable learning time, and the physical education teacher can use these times to maintain excellence in behavior. That excellence becomes a major means of managing people during their time together and, therefore, their effectiveness as a teacher.

CHAPTER 26

Incorporating Bullying Prevention in the Curriculu

Research reveals certain interesting elements associated with youth bullying that clarify both the occurrence and direction of the problem. Even though the problem of bullying decreases as students mature, it continues to exist in middle and high school classrooms, perhaps most extensively across all adolescent school ranks. Indications of bullying decrease if adult supervision, like teacher or parental advisory and involvement, is implemented; strategies are developed among peers who must interact with a loved acquaintance or ally; or students are feeling valued and skilled in utilizing protective factors. Since the early grades teach these respectful and protective elements through their hidden nuances, imagine how students' behavior would improve if formal bullying procedures were developed in the classroom to educate, practice, and enhance skill strengths developed in the home curriculum. Such procedures continue to reach all six grades by protecting young adolescents through necessary coaching or mature involvement for a brightened future.

How do we, as educators, make an impact on our school family community in order to avoid the chaos of the event described above or countless others that go unnoticed? What steps must be taken to ensure that this aspect of trouble associated with adolescents in all walks of life is an exception rather than an expectation? Schools and classrooms are microcosms of the global community in which students are privy to the social universes within and beyond their doors remotely. These worlds often embody a culture filled with relationships that epitomize the character of our society and occasionally reflect "clear-sighted perceptions that strengthen and unify opposing individuals to achieve common goals."

CHAPTER 27

Using Technology to Address Bullying

The Tyler Clementi Foundation, established following the death of Rutgers College freshman Tyler Clementi, who committed suicide after being bullied online, provides support and resources to counteract and address cyberbullying and harassment, as well as to identify and celebrate acts of kindness, promote safe, inclusive and respectful social, physical and educational environments, and increase education and awareness to help end this heartbreak. The foundation addresses the unique challenges of cyberbullying by recruiting artists, technologists, and parents with connections in business, including the technology sector, to develop platforms for student audiences. It uses visual storytelling to address bullying's multiple challenges. Both traditional and social media are used to engage this powerful and effective outlet for communicating with students and the public in general. The foundation also provides training for parents and educators, and activities that encourage young people to support one another and themselves when they witness online negativity.

Technology, it seems, is becoming a driving force behind many of today's society's ills, especially bullying. Research indicates that most

American teenagers use technology to communicate, some of it 24/7, which, in part, makes the digital world the place where they are most likely to be bullied. Of course, technology also connects people in ways never imagined before and, while it can be a breeding ground for bullying behavior, it also holds the potential to empower many to face and overcome the bullying in their lives. This duality offers new, innovative, and exciting opportunities to address bullying, opportunities which may very well be more effective than yesterday's solutions.

CHAPTER 28

Empowering Student Leaders

Although most classroom teachers realize that they have a responsibility for educating, preparing and nurturing their students for independence, that responsibility does not traditionally extend to safety and security. Unfortunately, many students who are shy, short or overweight are common targets of bullies. Using principles of positive reinforcement can prevent, reduce or help control this type of incident. Whether the reinforcement involves a sticker or a whole-class celebration of the individuality and talent of the targeted student, recognizing these students is a group effort which maintains and promotes a culture that is kind, fair and respectful of others. To achieve this deadline for the classroom as a safe, peaceful place is unlikely. Teachers can, however, support students who are involved in creating such a classroom. With guidance and support, the students can work together to earn and keep respect as well as rewards for safety, consideration and productivity.

The multiple modalities for promoting and practicing the safe school model should be applied in a form that broadens the responsibility for maintaining safety and security to include all students. Involving students in the process of maintaining a school safe from violence can have a significant effect. As student Fraser reported, administrators, district safety officers, and law enforcement's response to fighting was not ideally effective. In the long run, what made a difference in his school were programs that build self-confidence and respect among students and contribute to teamwork to keep inappropriate face-to-face physical interactions from escalating. Featherstone Middle School in Orangevale, CA implemented a formal program designed to promote student leadership and student ownership of the success and security of the school in 2000. That same year, although it has problems with fighting, bullying, verbal threats and vandalism, the number of discipline referral incidents was 13 percent lower than the previous 4 year average.

CHAPTER 29

Evaluating and Monitoring Bullying Prevention Effo

In their extreme form, such bully-proofing evaluations are often mistakenly reduced to the administration of school-wide, classroom-based, and other periodic surveys of anonymous student perceptions of school and classroom climates, anonymous teacher perceptions of similar issues, and anonymous parent perceptions of the school's social climate. These evaluations, whose results are usually posted, must be based on a sufficiently comprehensive theoretical system to avoid both an eventual backlash against bullying prevention efforts and more than a school can afford. Bottlenecks caused by efforts that are slipping through a narrow channel. The issue is that both prevention initiatives and evaluation of their efforts in micro terms must be based on assessment models that allow broad schools, with diverse community and staff capacities, to exhibit impacts that are meaningful to all.

Vigilant and active monitoring is essential in maintaining a safe, nurturing environment. Reliable procedures to ensure that ongoing evaluations of effectiveness of programs and policies to deter bullying are essential, as is the systematic documentation of what programs and practices are effective in creating bully-proof environments. It is true that these procedures may be costly and that ongoing quantitative evaluations may be very time-consuming; it is true that they might sometimes be more destructive than beneficial. Nevertheless, it is essential that schools continue to pursue efficient and unobtrusive assessment methods that accurately document the extent to which individual and systemic bullying prevention programs and practices are effective.

CHAPTER 30

Celebrating Diversity and Inclusion

In his book, Embracing Disabilities in the Classroom: Strategies to Maximize Students' Assets, author Jeffrey L. Coney expresses the viewpoint that any disability within a community is everyone's responsibility. This includes the responsibility to understand, respect and most of all include all persons in everyday activities. Creating a culture of respect that includes every individual by exposing students and educators to the needs of all unique types of people is the tent-pole goal of any effective "Disability Awareness Week" that extends far beyond the walls of a school. This week should be successful because people recognize the equal need for respect for all other individuals. The mark of a successful awareness week is educating educators to treat everyone's individual accomplishments as unique signs of beauty woven through the fabric of each person's life in any place of prestige and in the classroom. Like any other piece of fabric, there is no substitute for this unique strength. When we as educators display and respect everyone's individual value, student bullying vanishes and is no longer a problem of prevalent concern. The age-old philosophy of "every person possesses their unique strengths" invites everyone to respectfully engage in conversations with everyone to create educational and societal communities. This vision, with our schools as the creator and provider of change, will not only reduce barriers, but also introduce more frictionless positive social outcomes.

Has your school ever hosted "Disability Awareness Week"? During this week, all people focus on an unlimited respect for the individual and sharing our accomplishments with one another. We understand the emotional and tangible benefits of recognizing people's abilities and accomplishments while we conduct in-depth discussions about students' needs within the school environment and stress the shared need for respect for all persons. "Thank You" banners in the hallways or lanyards indicating our level of commitment to organizations are the marks of any successful "Awareness Week." Yet, as the sun set on that particular awareness week, we sunk back into our normal weekday routine, most of us leaving our newly acquired sensitivity toward individual need in the dressers of our locked school lockers.

CHAPTER 31

Promoting a Culture of Respect

In a school, as in all effective moral communities, the first value to be cherished and the first to be practiced is "respect" for oneself and respect for others, by which I mean not only respecting others who are like you but respecting others who are different. How can we in a school teach urban children to be both comfortable and civilized in a world where about one fifth of those they respect and learn to work with are people brought up in a different religion, totally different moral conventions, and view of the world? One answer, I think, is to begin by insisting on one great discipline that schools can teach and that is "the discipline of paying attention." For 20 years as a college teacher, I have been trying to teach my students the simple but very hard lesson that you must do the very hard work of understanding other people's ideas and the best and the profoundest way to do that is through deep exposure to literature, art, and music. This is how you truly become a cosmopolitan citizen.

Without a doubt, one of your most sacred obligations to the world and the future is to prepare your children, your own children, to meet the challenges of citizenship and to help them acquire the knowledge, the skills, and the wisdom they will need. In other words, what the ancient Greeks called paideia, education in the largest sense. Now to do that, the schools our children attend, indeed even more, the environments in which they live, have to be places where traditional values are cherished and imparted, like realizing our obligations to others, taking careful thought. If modern society, the society represented in this auditorium, if it is to survive what the ancient Greeks knew as anagke, absolute necessity, then we have to rebuild strong moral communities. Now how do we do that?

CHAPTER 32

Conclusion

This blueprint is both feasible and enjoyable. By reducing overt and covert bullying, both victim and bully truancy, drug use, and criminal behavior, and dropout and pregnancy, the bully-proof classroom increases the safety and the joy of being in school. Where the bully-proof classroom is grounded in a conviction that participation is a human right, and a scientifically credible determination that voice and friendship prevent acts of genocidal scale, the bully-proof classroom is an educational imperative. Character education, sociomoral education, service learning, and responsive classroom are not antifreeze for the pursuit of mathematical and verbal literacy. They are as necessary as grammar or multiplication for ethical literacy, the literacy of power and fellowship through principled negotiation with others.

I began the exploration of the bully-proof classroom with a challenge to rethink our approach to bullying. I suggested that punitive approaches often entrench the dynamic of bullying power, and that compassion based first on respect, and then on rigorous expectations for conscientious and ethical behavior, are more effective. If this has been a compelling assumption for you, then the chapters of this book have proposed a practical and robust blueprint for a classroom culture of respect. This blueprint includes explicit and redundant opportunities for teaching, modeling, checking, and celebrating a respect for people. It includes time for reflection and dialogue about issues of respect and responsibility. It includes repeated opportunities for collaborating to make choices that both parties will respect, and thus for developing an ethical knowledge by doing, and for increasing competence in principled negotiation. Competence and practice with principled negotiation are powerful antidotes to covert bullying, or to unprincipled scrapping and fighting, and they protect the asymmetric relationship structure of simple peer mediation.

Milton Keynes UK
Ingram Content Group UK Ltd.
UKHW031054291124
451807UK00006B/474